THIS BOOK BELONGS TO

For Gavin and my three reds.
Thank you for all your love and support.
-MB

Text by Mande Buckmaster
Illustration by Jessica Chrysler
Copyright © 2018 Mande Buckmaster

Buckmaster, Mande, author
Title: Your Greatest Adventure / Mande Buckmaster – First Edition.
Summary: Told in rhyme, a fearless adventurer (typical toddler) discovers the greatest adventure of all.
ISBN 978-1-7320568-0-0 (hardcover) – ISBN 978-1-7320568-1-7 (paperback) – ISBN 978-1-7320568-2-4 (ebook)
[1. Stories in Rhyme. 2. Parent and child–Fiction. 3. Adventure–Fiction.]

Available in hardcover, paperback, and e-book.
Creative Ambition Press

YOUR GREATEST Adventure

Avery,
Cheers to all

♡ - Mande
MB

You are
= the Greatest
adventure! ♥

MANDE BUCKMASTER
ART BY JESSICA CHRYSLER

You love adventures, it's easy to see.

Bet you didn't know you got that from me.

We both crave big thrills, and hunt to find more.

Adventures aplenty roar shore to shore!

Tell me! Tell me! What things will I do?
I want to find adventures with you.

You'll pilot a plane, way up in the air.

Like a bird through the clouds, you'll soar up there.

You'll feel almost weightless gliding above...

...Over the people and places, you love.

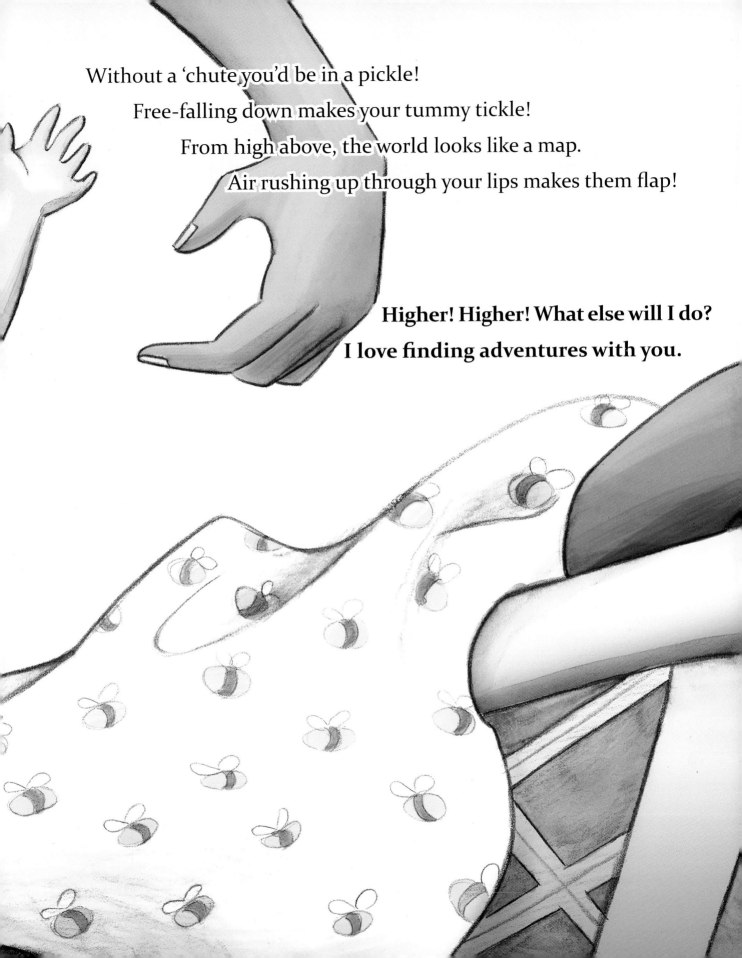

Without a 'chute you'd be in a pickle!

Free-falling down makes your tummy tickle!

From high above, the world looks like a map.

Air rushing up through your lips makes them flap!

Higher! Higher! What else will I do?

I love finding adventures with you.

Drive a Jeep Wrangler through African Plains.

Take pictures of lions shaking their manes.

A cheetah will challenge you to a race...

...To show off the fastest pace in the place.

Chase a tornado to walk through its eye.
Swirling around you, it blocks out the sky.
You'll dodge flying objects like cows and trees,
Twirling around you like a swarm of bees.

Faster! Faster! What else will I do?
I love finding adventures with you.

Float through the sky without steering or brakes...

Over great mountains, cities, and lakes.

Up, up you'll climb using wind and fire...

...To blow your balloon and send you higher.

Grab onto the saddle and hold on tight.
That bucking bronco will put up a fight!
You'll "Cowboy Up" to keep your hat on straight.
Throw your hand in the air and count to eight!

Yee-haw! Yee-haw! What else will I do?
I love finding adventures with you.

Your fingers hold cracks for balance and grip.

Your strong legs and back assure you won't slip.

You'll use a sure foot to get to the top.

Up, over boulders -keep climbing, don't stop!

Then strap yourself in and dangle down rocks.

While others look on, scared out of their socks.

The trick is to not chance a downward glance.

So, back up and shuffle, like a tap dance.

Awesome! Awesome! What else will I do?
I love finding adventures with you.

Zip into a jump suit, fit for a clown.

Scream your head off the entire way down.

When the bungee bounces you back up top,

"AGAIN!" You'll say, and never want to stop!

White water raft over rapids and falls.

Don't ignore Mother Nature when she calls!

Currents and waves toss and turn you with might.

You'll paddle hard, hitting the surge just right!

Paddle! Paddle! What else will I do?

I love finding adventures with you.

Throw out a line in the deep ocean blue,
And reel in a fish much bigger than you.
Holding the line as a mighty marlin fights
Certainly wins you a few bragging rights!

Dive into the deep and swim with Great Whites.

In a cage, of course, you wouldn't want bites!

As big sharks circle, so close you could kiss...

You'll think there's no thrill to ever beat this.

Again! Again! What else will I do?

I love finding adventures with you.

Exploring the world, so near and so far...

...You'll seek adventures by plane, boat and car.

Your passport stamps will record every place

Where adventures and fun made your heart race.

One day you'll find the adventures you did,

Are twice the delight when you have a kid.

I know for a fact that all this is true...

My greatest adventure clearly is you.